Creative Incarnations

Alison Grills

BookLeaf
Publishing

India | USA | UK

Presentation by *BookLeaf Publishing*

Web: www.bookleafpub.com

E-mail: info@bookleafpub.com

ISBN: 978-93-5744-994-6

First edition 2022

DEDICATION

To the many people who have inspired me over the years.

In particular my partner in life - you know who you are.

PREFACE

I came up with the title of this book a long time ago. It came from the idea that instead of the "word made flesh", my experiences as a human being have been distilled down into poetry form.

I've been writing poetry since I was a kid. It often helped me process emotions I had difficulty expressing in other ways. As a bonus it also works as a journal, as I can track the changes in the way I express myself over time. I've added notes along the way about how I think I've developed in the way I see myself and the world around me.

The first poem I remember writing was at the age of seven. I am now 48. That's a lot of years of writing my thoughts and feelings down. It hasn't been a consistent process. I was much more prolific in my teens and early twenties. Recently I have been trying to reignite the spark.

This anthology covers a lot of topics, some personal, some just for fun. There is quite a lot around mental health as that is something I have struggled with for most of my life. My hope is that it helps people who have been there to know they are not alone. For those who haven't, I hope it creates some sense of perspective, and reduces the stigma that still surrounds mental illness.

The poems Moments and Beyond the Cocoa Bean have been previously published in Beyond the Tobacco Bush, Beyond The Cocoa Bean by Ginninderra Press in 2003.

Beauty

Tears blur her vision
She cannot see the beauty
That lies all around

So young it seems strange
That there is so much pain
Already weighing down her heart

She needs someone to reach out
Hold her hand, comfort her
She needs someone to help her
See the beauty in herself

Authors Notes:
I was in my early teens when I wrote this. I'm
actually pretty impressed by my own insight.

Words

Words that rhyme, words that scan,
Words with flowing rhythm.
Words that paint pictures clear,
Convey the writer's image.

Goodness or evil, thoughts and fears,
Sweet dreams or nasty nightmares,
Poems, words, ideas revealed,
Imaginations brain-child.

Authors Notes:
There is a lot to be said for putting words to
paper. The process can be very cathartic,
especially when you don't feels safe to say some
of those things out loud. It helped me so much
through my youth, I feel like it would help just
as much now. Which is why am trying to bring it
back into my life again in a meaningful way.
This journey back through my memories is in
part an attempt to reignite my muse.

But

I don't like crowds
But I feel hurt when I'm left out
I like to be alone
But I get lonely, so easily
I don't accept many invitations
But feel rejected when they're not issued
I'm a walking contradiction
But...that doesn't make much sense.

Authors Notes:
This is a pretty good summary of living with
anxiety that hasn't been diagnosed. Wanting
social interaction but also being overwhelmed
by it. I lived like that for a long time. These days
I know why I feel the way I do, and once I find a
place or person I feel safe with, you actually
can't shut me up.

Music my life

Music my life, my life is music,
Without it I'd hardly survive.
No matter what happens, good things or bad,
It can make me feel glad I'm alive.

Dancing or singing, to songs or just tunes,
It can cure my every frustration.
Moving to music, move to the beat,
Of humankind's greatest creation.

Pain or sorrow, lethargy, grief,
Music can cure me of all.
Any affliction, I feel I can beat,
With music I will never fall.

Authors Notes:
I got my first LP at age eleven. Since then music
has been my best way to get out of my head, lift
my mood, raise my energy, and generally make
everything better. I honestly think it helped me

survive my adolescence, and still gets me
through the bad days even now.

5

Individuals

We are animals of unknown species
Becoming extinct, not many survive
We fight to exist in this world of so-called
"NORMAL PEOPLE"
But our ideas and ideals differ so much
We are often misunderstood
Our kind stick together
There's safety in numbers
But still we are vulnerable
Easily hurt
We're often thought weird
And mocked by our peers
But we keep trying
Hoping, that someday
We'll be accepted for what we are

Authors Notes:
I have always found this particular poem
especially poignant. The sense of otherness, not
fitting in. Being singled out for any difference.
But at the same time realising that you don't

want to be like everyone else, if being like
everyone else means not being yourself. It was a
pretty big turning point for me. What I didn't
know then was that more of us feel that way
than I could ever have imagined.

Unicorns

Unearthly creatures of ethereal beauty
No-one may see them save those who are pure
In legend and fancy they were created
Can one ever explain their magical lure?
Over and over their mysteries enchant me
Real or imagined? Extinct or alive?
Now and again I feel they protect me
Safeguarding my dreams so that they may thrive

Authors Notes:
This might seem out of place, but my love for
this particular mythical beast really did help me
in so many ways. My brother gave me a baby
unicorn ornament for my twelfth birthday, and it
was love at first sight. I have been collecting
them ever since. It started my love of fantasy in
general, books, movies, art, and is a great way to
escape my world when I need a break.

Survivor

Behind the tears she sheds
The desperation to be loved
The loneliness that overwhelms
There lies a hidden strength

She will always be a survivor
No matter what life throws her way
But she feels the time has come
To do much more than just survive

If only there was half a chance
That things could really go her way
And her hopes reach their fruition
Instead of dying half-way through

How can she change the bad luck
And have good things within her reach
How can she change her fortune
And succeed despite the odds

If somebody out there could answer her question
If someone could help make her life more
worthwhile
If they would love her, and want her with them
Then perhaps the survivor could finally thrive

I'm noticing a theme. I was very focused on someone outside helping me out of the hole I was in. Which was fair enough, I was young and didn't have the skills or experience to help myself. These days I know it's about seeking help not waiting for someone else to magically appear. There are still days when it's so exhausting just existing that I feel that desire for someone else to just take over, and finding people who are willing to support me in my darkest moments is essential, but it will ultimately always be up to me.

Question Mark

You say you don't really know
How you feel about me.
Feelings hidden for so long,
Are now so hard to find.

You know how much I love you,
But don't know how to take it.
You show me sweet affection,
But who knows if it's real.

Deep down, I believe you care for me,
I see it in your actions.
But when it comes to words not deeds,
You can't confirm my hopes.

When I watch you watching me,
Your eyes seem to betray you.
They speak of love and trusting,
Can it really be a lie?

Perhaps I'll never really know,
What lies behind your silence.
And the feelings I think I see,
Will elude me ever more.

But if someday you can trust me,
With the depths of your emotions,
I'll keep them safe within my heart,
Where you already are.

Authors Notes:
This was written in the early stages of my
relationship with the man who would become
my husband. The eerie thing is it could have
been written today. We've only recently
discovered my partner is on the Autism
Spectrum and that difficulty identifying and
expressing emotions is part and parcel. But now
just as then if you look at actions instead of
words, he shows me how much he cares every
day.

Panic

Heat rising
Face flushing
Skin burning
Throat tightening
Ears ringing
Head throbbing
Mind spinning
Nerves prickling
Heart racing
Blood pounding
Lungs straining
Stomach clenching
Limbs trembling
Muscles screaming

Have to fight have to flee
This death grip of anxiety
Eyes searching desperately
For the terror stalking me
But there is nothing to see
The dread beast lurks
Inside of me

Moments

A green secluded spot,
trees spaced apart so that sunlight
and shade dapple the ground.
The blue sky populated here and
there with high white clouds.

The murmur of the ocean,
viewed through a gap in the grassy bank,
white foam tips against the horizon
as the tide moves towards the shore.

Bird songs, twitters and chirps
as the little ones flit amongst the trees.
Larger birds, wings spread wide,
float on the breeze like gliders.

A rug, a picnic lunch,
my love sitting by my side.
Breathe in the warm sea scented air,
close my eyes and listen to
nature's soothing rhythm.
Midday sun on my back, relax.
In this moment, everything is perfect.

Authors Notes:

This was an attempt to capture a single moment in time. For the most part perfection is an unattainable goal, but it turns out if you're open to it, you might just recognise it in fleeting instances of everything being just right just then.

Goodbye

While death always bring sorrow,
when it creeps up unawares,
it leaves those left behind
with a heavy load to bear.

When the loss of a loved one,
has come as a surprise,
then often friends and family
don't have time to say good-bye.

At least not while the person,
can hear you, and reply,
or for you to hold their hand,
and look into their eyes.

There's nothing to let you know,
that you've been heard and understood,
that they know how much you loved them,
and that you always would.

That they know that you are sorry,
if you ever did them wrong,
or regret taking for granted,
that they'd just keep going strong.

You will often wish that you
had one last chance to let them know,
how glad you are they were part of your life,
and that you will miss them so.

But one day, as time passes,
you'll be able to let go,
and be certain, somehow, in your heart,
that they already know.

Authors Notes:
Just when things seemed to be going better, I
was engaged due to be married the following
year, I was in the last year of my Diploma in
Welfare Studies, a somewhat normal life seemed
within reach. Then my father died of a sudden
major heart attack. I was 25, Dad was only 60.
My relationship with my Dad had always been
tricky. I loved him with all my heart but there
were also times I was very afraid of him. I didn't
know at the time how much my mental health
played a part in that dichotomy. What I did
figure out, thankfully before we lost him, was
that Dad was a human being, capable of both
good and bad, of making mistakes and hopefully

learning from them. Once he stopped being a
larger than life figure our relationship became
more stable. I wish I'd had more time with him
after that realisation, but I will be forever
grateful that it didn't come too late.

Snapshot

A playground seen in the fading light
of a winter sunset
A grown woman clambers over the structure
reliving the joys of childhood, see-saws and
slippery-dips

Wearing jeans, sneakers and a warm jacket
her hair is blown a bit in the breeze
Her cheeks are flushed, her eyes sparkling
She flashes her teeth in a spontaneous grin

Her partner is there, indulging her playfulness
but not joining in her glee
She hands him a camera
wanting to capture the moment

Up and down on the see-saw, a breathless giggle
SNAP – saved forever

Standing at the top of the slide
wondering if her womanly hips will fit
on this child's toy - They do!
She settles herself, smiling broadly
arms flung out to embrace the world
SNAP

The shutter clicks seconds before
she pushes herself off and slides to the bottom
then bounces up again, looking around
for what to do next

The light is almost gone
and the wind blows colder
Time to leave

She follows her partner to the waiting car
looks back at the playground with longing
and wonders how the photos will turn out

Authors Notes:
This one dates itself to the early noughties by the
use of a digital camera rather than a smartphone.
It's another poem about appreciating those brief
but precious moments of joy. For me it is also
very much about holding on to the ability to be
playful, something we tend to lose as we get
older. I live by the quote "Growing older is
mandatory, growing up is optional."

Too Much

Just too much to think about
Way too much to feel
Too many demands on me
Some perceived, but mostly real

Too much to get my head around
Too hard to come to terms
It seems impossible to have
the rest for which my body yearns

'They need me' is the constant thought
'I just can't let them down'
So I go and go and only slow
When ill health forces me to ground

But the cycle soon starts up again
All before I'm fully well
So by day I try my best to cope
And by night, my dreams go straight to hell

Authors Notes:

Despite losing Dad being such a blow, I really did think I was making progress. I had developed coping strategies, I'd accepted that I was weird and that was okay. I tried to live the life I thought was expected of me. Studying, working, volunteering, trying to maintain a social life and personal relationships. But I was still living with complex chronic physical and mental health issues that were still mostly undiagnosed or poorly managed. It was too much. I hit the wall. It actually felt like I hit the wall and then the wall fell on me. The one potential positive that came out of it was once all my coping strategies crumbled and just how unwell I really was laid bare, I finally got the diagnosis that would make a big difference to my understanding of myself and my past.

Somewhere

Somewhere round the world there's people fighting,
Every week of every year.
Somewhere round the world there's people dying,
And people living their lives in fear.

Hatred and destruction are everywhere,
It seems nowhere's safe any more.
The fighting gets worse, the weapons more dangerous,
But I'd like to know what they're all fighting for.

Each side wants to win but that just can't be,
'Cause each side loses more than they gain.
As they send home their wounded and dead men,
The blind, crippled and insane.

Still the fighting continues never seeming to stop.
And the killing just goes on and on.
Can something be done to end this nightmare?
If not, soon we may all be gone.

Authors Notes:

Everything so far has been very inward looking. I did also have some pretty strong feelings about the outside world. This was written during the Cold War with the whole mutually assured destruction thing hanging over our heads. I was still too young to understand a lot, but I understood enough to be genuinely afraid.

Ghosts

Shadows of what was
Echoes of pain and fear
That reverberate through time

Trauma stamped on the souls of survivors
Passed down through generations

Cracks in the psyche
That can never be plastered over
Or repainted to make them new

Scars on the landscape still felt
Long after the rebuilding is complete

A dark energy that lingers
Marring the atmosphere
A bloody X marking the spot

You might ask me if I believe
I don't just believe, I know

These ghosts are with us always
In the corner of our eyes or our minds
Our world is built on the bodies of those left
behind

Authors Notes:
This one is a new poem, inspired by photos of regional France before and after the destruction of World War I. It was written days before the 20th anniversary of 9/11 and I was shaken by how easily it could have been written for that instead.

New Neighbours

Into my house enters a large
Octopus almost the size of a barge
Slinking across the hardwood floor
Leaving slime, seaweed and more

What are you doing? I cried in disbelief
Don't you need water to get some relief?
I tipped out the flowers right over its head
Worried that if they dried out they'd be dead

Suddenly the thought occurred to me
Perhaps it was my life for which I should flee
But now the wood floor was both slimy and wet
My act of kindness I did now regret

Don't fear, said the octopus, I'm not your foe
Seriously I'm just an average Joe
With sea levels rising so fast and so high
Us being neighbours was drawing quite nigh

I thought that I would get ahead of the crowd
Interspecies mingling can be really loud
So Hi there neighbour, I'm pleased to meet you
I'll be here to help when we're all in the stew

Authors Notes:

A bit of light relief, sort of. Another new poem, a writing exercise that actually really spoke to me. It may be humorous but it still invokes the latest existential crisis we face as human beings. For someone living with anxiety to begin with, it can be a lot to take in.

Real Freaky

Turning knobs and rattling doors
Footsteps creak on empty floors
Temperatures jump from cold to hot
Things blown about when the window's shut
Heavy books thrown across the room
Midnight dreams of impending doom
Appliances act like they're possessed
Is this the sign of a soul's unrest?

We sense a boy not yet full grown
Who wants to make his presence known
We believe harm is not his intention
He's trying to get our full attention
Did something happen to him here
That brought him pain or caused him fear?
Or did he simply die too young
Before his life had yet begun?

The answer is a mystery
May be for all eternity
All we can do is try to calm
This spirit causing us alarm
This uncommon situation
Called for divine inspiration
These childish pranks have seemed to stall

Since the sainted mother adorned the wall

You may think this is a fairytale
Invented just to make you quail
But I tell you now, I speak the truth
And it happened under my own roof.

Authors Notes:
Yes, that is a true story, and no, I had not taken
anything hallucinogenic. I'm very glad another
person saw what I saw or I would have been
worried my various neuroses had made the leap
to psychosis. Some of it is poetic license. I don't
know who or what the presence was, but it was a
kids bedroom before we moved in. I am neither
a believer nor a skeptic when it comes to the
supernatural, but I do find it fascinating. I like to
think my Dad is still out there somewhere
keeping an eye on me. I guess we can't know
until we know, and nobody has come back to tell
the story.

Life in Pain

Muscles aching
Stretching, straining
Twisting, tearing
Pulling, spraining
Cramping, swelling
Tension, bunching
Stiffness, weakness
Spasms, hunching

Nerves tingling
Burning, itching
Stinging, screaming
Twinging, twitching
Searing, throbbing
Sharp and stabbing
Sudden, constant
Trapped and grabbing

Every movement is a test
Feel exhausted and fatigued
Mind won't give me peace or rest
Sometimes even hurts to breathe
Basic tasks take all I've got
No energy is left to spare
Freezing cold or stifling hot

My thermostat's in disrepair

Pain in all its forms and types
Level one through level ten
With me every day and night
Up and down and back again
Body parts all in the fray
Nothing spared the constant war
Psyche left in disarray
Wonder what I'm fighting for

Can't escape, no relief
Nothing seems to bring me ease
Taking all just like a thief
I'm left with nothing but dis-ease
Joy and laughter, what are they?
Safe and happy I am not
Good things have all gone away
I am left to grieve and rot

Depression and anxiety
Feeling frightened and alone
No place of haven or safety
Even tucked in bed at home
Not just another cry for help
Really wanted to end it all
So much suffering felt daily
Like a never ending fall

Authors Notes:

So, chronic pain. It really is a pain in the, well, everything. I was in the midst of one of the worst flares I had experienced and it was more than I could handle. I had experienced episodes of dark thoughts and urges from about the age of eleven, but this was next level. I really did get to a point that I couldn't imagine anything worse. Thankfully the mix of medication and therapies I use these days means that episodes that bad are fewer and further apart, but the fear of it still lingers.

Beyond The Cocoa Bean

Chocolate biscuits, chocolate bars
Arnotts, Nestle, Cadbury, Mars
Chocolate ice-cream, chocolate milk
Rich hot chocolate, smooth as silk

Dairy milk and sweetest white
Mouth watering at just the sight
Bitter dark, assorted creams
Fill a chocoholics dreams

Streets and Roses, Whitmans, Dove
Feels just like first flush of love
Energy boost, endorphin high
Sugar levels reach the sky

Blood sugar spikes mean sudden drops
The happy buzz abruptly stops
Chemical bliss can never last
Too soon, we feel once more downcast

Chocolate can help to ease the strain
When it's just too hard to face the pain

But it can't alter the basic fact
That those feelings will always come back

There has to be a better way
To get us through our darkest day
We might discover something real
If we stop masking how we feel

This path is only for the brave
It's hard to give up what you crave
And I must admit, with much regret
Though I'm trying, I am not there yet

Authors Notes:
In a cruel irony I am now allergic (or at least intolerant) to most chocolate. Kinder is about the only thing that is still safe, and it's not even mentioned in the poem. Using short term "feel good" options, of any kind, can help you survive the worst moments, but if you become too reliant they become their own problem. I am trying hard to use strategies like relaxation or mindfulness exercises more often, but as the poem says, I am not there yet.

Intervention

Life & death choices
Made every day
To be or not be
Leave this world or stay

How can we help them
See there is light
The tunnel's not endless
Life is worth the fight

Maybe we can't
Is it too much to ask?
Should we set ourselves
A more realistic task

Get through the moment
The hour, the week
Press the pause button
Just get past dangers peak

For each extra second
Someone stays alive
Gives them one more chance
To find a way to survive

Authors Notes:

I mentioned a couple of poems ago getting to a point that I couldn't imagine anything worse. The biggest hurdle is getting someone back to a place where they can start to imagine things getting better. Chronic physical and mental health issues are both episodic. Sometimes things will be unbearable, but eventually it will pass. Unfortunately that means that when things are actually going pretty well, that will also pass. My counsellor has me working on something called radical acceptance. Knowing that life will sometimes really suck and you can't control that, but you can survive it. It's a big ask. Give me time.

It's Time

It is time to make a statement,
Time to take a chance,
March to the beat of a different drum,
Do a different kind of dance.

Find your place in society,
And your place in the world.
Not where others expect you to be,
But where your own flag can be unfurled.

Time to be your own person,
Follow the road of your choice,
Time to stand up and be counted,
Time to find your own voice.

Take the time to know yourself,
The real you deep inside,
Learn to love the person you are,
And there will be no need to hide.

I know it's easier said than done,
But now's the time to take your cue,
Taking control of your life can be tough,
But if I can do it so can you!

Authors Notes:

Chronologically this poem is very out of place, but I wanted my book to have a happy ending. It was written during one of the rare moments when I really felt that I had a handle on things and the only way was up. Realistically life is more like a roller-coaster. There are ups, there are downs, there are stomach churning twists and turns. The thing I have learnt, following that theme, is that closing your eyes, clutching hard to the safety bar and screaming, doesn't really help. When you watch what's coming, and try to prepare for it, and are willing to put your hand(s) up when necessary, you've got a better chance of it being an enjoyable ride.